T0051057

WORLD'S WORST NATURAL DISASTERS

THE WORLD'S WORST
TSUNAMIS

by Tracy Nelson Maurer

CAPSTONE PRESS
a capstone imprint

Blazers Books are published by Capstone Press,
1710 Roe Crest Drive, North Mankato, Minnesota 56003
www.mycapstone.com

Library of Congress Cataloging-in-Publication Data is available on the Library
of Congress website.
ISBN: 978-1-5435-5478-6 (library hardcover) — 978-1-5435-5902-6
(paperback) — 978-1-5435-5482-3 (eBook PDF)

Summary: Learn about the most devastating tsunamis in history.

Editorial Credits
Gena Chester, editor; Juliette Peters, designer; Jo Miller,
media researcher; Tori Abraham, production specialist

Photo Credits
Alamy: Chronicle, 14–15, FLHC 46, 18–19, North Wind Picture Archives,
10–11; Bridgeman Images: Look and Learn/Private Collection, 12–13;
Getty Images: Bettmann/Contributor, 22–23, De Agostini Picture
Library, 16–17; Newscom: MCT/Handout, 20–21, ZUMA Press/
Jana/Air Photo Service, 8–9; Shutterstock: Christian Vinces, 4–5,
Frans Delian, 6–7, leonello calvetti, Cover, 3, 31, mTaira, Cover,
Sundry Photography, 28–29, Tuah Roslan, 26–27; Wikimedia: UBC
Library, 24–25

Design Elements
Shutterstock: irynal, Ivana Milic, xpixel

TABLE OF CONTENTS

KILLER WAVES

Water at the beach rushes out to sea. The seawater gathers into huge waves that speed toward shore. It's a **tsunami**! Tsunamis often follow earthquakes. A volcanic eruption, underwater **landslide**, or **meteor** impact can start the killer waves too.

tsunami—gigantic ocean wave created by an undersea earthquake, landslide, or volcanic eruption

Tsunami is a Japanese word: *Tsu* means "harbor" and *nami* means "wave."

landslide—a large mass that suddenly slides down a mountain or hill

meteor—a piece of rock that burns up as it passes through Earth's atmosphere

THE DEADLIEST TSUNAMI

Location:
Sumatra, Indonesia

Date:
December 26, 2004

Estimated Damage:
$10 Billion

$$$$$
$$$$$

$ = one billion dollars

One sunny day, a huge earthquake cracked the ocean floor near Sumatra. Waves reaching 100 feet tall (30 meters) rushed to the shore. The deadly tsunami hit 14 countries. At least 225,000 people died.

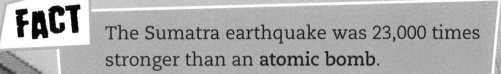

FACT

The Sumatra earthquake was 23,000 times stronger than an **atomic bomb**.

atomic bomb—a powerful bomb that explodes with great force, heat, and bright light

JAPAN'S MONSTER TSUNAMI

Location:
Tohoku, Japan

Date:
March 11, 2011

Estimated Damage:
$300 Billion

$$$

$ = one hundred billion dollars

Japan's strongest earthquake caused a monster tsunami. Water plowed 6 miles (10 kilometers) inland and hit a nuclear power plant. Almost 16,000 people died. Deadly **radiation** filled the area. No one can safely live there for many years.

FACT

Japan's 2011 tsunami waves traveled about 500 miles per hour (800 km per hour). That's about as fast as an airplane.

WAVES OF TERROR

Location:
Lisbon, Portugal

Date:
November 1, 1755

A series of earthquakes hit Lisbon, Portugal, in 1755. Churches crumpled and fallen candles spread fires. Survivors ran to the shore. But minutes later, a 20-foot (6-m) wave hit the town. Two more waves followed. About 60,000 people died.

The Lisbon tsunami waves reached as far as Africa and the Caribbean.

ERUPTION AND DESTRUCTION

Location:
Krakatau,
Indonesia

Date:
August 27, 1883

In 1883, in Indonesia, three volcanic eruptions roared one after another. It was the loudest sound ever in modern history. Deadly tsunami waves followed. The water was as high as an 11-story building. More than 36,000 people died.

Tsunamis have happened in every ocean on Earth.

DOUBLE WHAMMY

Location:
Arica, Peru
(present-day Chile)

Date:
August 13, 1868

Estimated Damage:
$400–$800 million

$$$$–
$$$$
$$$$

$ = one
hundred
million dollars

Twin earthquakes shook the ocean floor near present-day Chile. The two quakes caused one powerful tsunami. The waves traveled more than 10,000 miles (17,000 km) to Japan! The disaster killed more than 25,000 people.

FACT

The tsunami waves traveled across the ocean for three days.

SURPRISE LANDSLIDE

Location:
Messina, Italy

Date:
December 28, 1908

In 1908, an underwater landslide in Italy caused a killer tsunami. In moments, waves raced into Italian towns. No one was ready. Water crushed buildings. The tsunami killed more than 80,000 people.

FACT

Rescuers pulled two children alive from the **rubble** 18 days after the tsunami.

rubble—things such as bricks and concrete left from a building that has fallen down

WORLD'S TALLEST TSUNAMI

Location:
Lituya Bay,
Alaska

Date:
July 9, 1958

**Estimated
Damage:**
$1 Million

$

$ = one million
dollars

In 1958 an earthquake broke off part of a cliff above a bay in Alaska. The huge landslide charged into the sea. Its impact caused a deadly splash tsunami. The wave reached 1,740 feet (530 m) high.

FACT

The 1958 Alaska tsunami wiped away thousands of trees.

THE GREAT ALASKAN TSUNAMI

Location:
Gulf of Alaska

Date:
March 27, 1964

Estimated Damage:
$311 Million

$$$$$
$$$$$
$$$$

$ = one hundred million dollars

$ = one million dollars

In 1964 another tsunami hit Alaska. One of the world's biggest earthquakes caused it. More than 130 people died. Waves pulsed across the entire Pacific Ocean all the way to the gulf!

TSUNAMI ZONE

Location:
Hilo, Hawaii

Date:
April 1, 1946

Estimated Damage:
$300 Million

$$$

$ = one hundred million dollars

One of the worst tsunamis to hit Hawaii rolled across the Pacific Ocean from Alaska. Powerful waves pushed houses into other buildings. **Debris**-filled water claimed 159 lives.

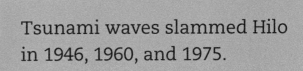

debris—the pieces of something that has been broken

TWIN TSUNAMIS

Location:
Sanriku, Japan

Date:
June 15, 1896

An earthquake off the coast of Japan caused two tsunamis in 1896. The first topped 124 feet (38 m). About 22,000 people died. Soon after the first wave, another smaller tsunami roared into China. The second round killed 4,000 people.

Scientists still use records from the Sanriku tragedy to study tsunamis.

WATER WORK

Scientists want to learn how to better **predict** tsunamis. Ocean **buoys** track sea level changes. **Tsunameters** check the ocean floor for even the smallest movements. These could signal an earthquake or other tsunami **trigger**.

predict—to say what will happen in the future

buoy—a floating marker in the ocean

tsunameter—equipment that detects tsunamis

trigger—an event or situation that causes something else

Not every earthquake causes a tsunami. But it's hard to know which earthquake will send a wall of water to shore. The U.S. government created TsunamiReady® Guidelines for people who live near the ocean. Some of the tips are:

1. After a strong earthquake, stay away from the coast.
2. Take any tsunami warning seriously.
3. If you live in a tsunami zone, create an escape plan.

FACT

A tsunami might follow a nearby earthquake in just minutes. Some traveling tsunamis take days to reach shore.

GLOSSARY

atomic bomb (uh-TOM-ik BOM)—a powerful bomb that explodes with great force, heat, and bright light

buoy (BOO-ee)—a floating marker in the ocean

debris (duh-BREE)—the pieces of something that has been broken

landslide (LAND-slyde)—a large mass that suddenly slides down a mountain or hill

meteor (MEE-tee-ur)—a piece of rock that burns up as it passes through Earth's atmosphere

predict (pri-DIKT)—to say what will happen in the future

radiation (ray-dee-AY-shuhn)—rays of energy given off by certain elements

rubble (RUB-uhl)—things like bricks and concrete left from a building that has fallen down

trigger (TRIG-uhr)—an event or situation that causes something else

tsunameter (tsoo-NAH-mee-tuhr)—equipment that detects tsunamis

tsunami (tsoo-NAH-mee)—a very large wave

READ MORE

Kopp, Megan. *Tsunamis*. Force of Nature. New York: Smartbook Media, Inc., 2018.

Meinking, Mary. *Natural Disasters*. Weather Watch. Minneapolis: Pop, 2018.

Squire, Ann O. *Tsunamis*. A True Book. New York: Children's Press, an imprint of Scholastic Inc., 2016.

INTERNET SITES

Use Facthound to find Internet sites related to this book.

Visit www.facthound.com.

Just type in 9781543554786 and go!

 Check out projects, games and lots more at **www.capstonekids.com**

CRITICAL THINKING QUESTIONS

1. What causes tsunamis?

2. Imagine you're at the beach. If you saw waves suddenly sucked back out to sea, what would you do?

3. Why do you think people run to higher ground after an earthquake?

INDEX